To order additional copies of this book for
family or friends (*delivered anonymously if
desired*), please visit our website at:

www.raisingalex.com

or send a check or money order for $14.95
plus $3.95 shipping and handling per copy to:

RAISING ALEX
7743 28th Avenue NW
Seattle, WA 98117

Please indicate ship-to address

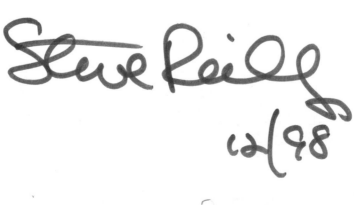

Steve Reilly
12/98

from Mary

Raising Alex

TEACHING A CHILD
TO MAKE SMART CHOICES

Steve Reilly

Foreword by Dr. John E. Felton, Ph.D.
University of Evansville

Printed in Canada
Cover Design by David Marty
Interior by Gopa Design

LCCCN: 98-067840
ISBN: 0-89716-817-8

PUBLISHED BY PEANUT BUTTER PUBLISHING
Pier 55, 1101 Alaskan Way, Suite 301
Seattle, WA 98101-2982
206-748-0345 • e-mail: pnutpub@aol.com
http://www.pbpublishing.com
Denver, Colorado • Scottsdale, Arizona
Portland, Oregon • Milwaukee, Wisconsin
Minneapolis/St.Paul, Minnesota
Vancouver, BC

For Astrid and Roger,
Alex's other parents

Acknowledgements

I want to thank a few special people...

Thanks Mom, for letting me sit in the front seat with you both to and from Mass each Sunday.

And thanks Dad, for your continued confidence in spite of all the mistakes you've watched me make.

Finally, thank you Elliott Bronstein.
Your help not only made this book better, it made me better.

Contents

Foreword

AHHH, "SMART CHOICES"—the stuff of which success-ful lives are made. I've known Steve Reilly for 26 years. In that time he has grown from a rather brash and superficial young man living pretty much for the moment, to a sensitive and insightful father. Somehow he developed the gift of extracting core truths from life's sit-uations and became a keen observer of human nature especially parenting behavior.

That he has taken the time to closely watch those around him is amazing considering the extremely suc-cessful career he sculpted out for himself as a corporate trainer. Steve is living proof that when motivated a per-son can find a healthy balance between career and family.

This apparent paradox of corporate player and percep-tive parent is perhaps the most surprising aspect of his book. On one hand Steve subscribes to the formula for business success in America today; work hard and focus on the variables one has control over. But in his personal life, he seems to be able rein in his urge to control realizing that his child must also have the freedom to make choices on her own. Steve appreciates that this potential conflict is only avoided by knowing where the subtle line exists between parental responsibility for protecting our children and allowing them to experience the consequences they must ultimately learn to live with.

It is difficult to communicate how impressed I am with this book. I have spent 20 years teaching psychology and 17 years working with families. My life has been dedicated to helping families function in a healthier way. In this book Steve takes some very elusive psychological concepts and presents them in a simple and meaningful manner. He distills ideas such as positive reinforcement, punishment, unconditional positive regard and others into a very readable and functional sharing of his personal observations over the first eight years of his daughters life.

Without any formal psychological training he gleaned from his personal and professional life the fact that people(including children) like to be in control of their futures. Therefore it makes sense to convey to our kids that their choices can determine much of their future.

Steve strikes a sensitive balance between the awesome responsibility of being a parent and the need for a young mind to become increasingly independent of parental control. He is also comfortable with the often touchy issue of mutual respect between parent and child.

Even with this insight Steve readily admits he is not the perfect parent. The soul searching he did to discover the things which worked is a process we all must go through if we are to be the best parents possible to our children. Almost as an aside he presents a blueprint for how estranged parents can and should work together to raise an emotionally healthy, responsible child even after the trauma of divorce.

On a larger scale Steve typifies a combination of several major schools of psychological thought. The behaviorist school will recognize the importance he places on being specific in communicating his expectations to Alex. He realizes that the clearer the choices are in Alex's mind, the more likely she is to pick the smart one.

The learning theorist in Steve knows that some of the most powerful lessons in Alex's life come from allowing her to experience the natural consequences of her choices.

And perhaps most importantly, Steve knows the power of love. His affection for Alex is evident in the pain it causes him. Watching his daughter struggle with the frustration and disappointment caused by the necessary limits he imposes is a challenge all parents must face.

Finally, he is a humanist. Steve has confidence in Alex's ability, and by inference man's ability, to make good decisions and ultimately solve the problems life presents.

Parents and parents-to-be will learn from Steve and Alex's journey. His philosophy of using both rational analysis and deep love is necessary to raise a responsible child. This book can help us all fulfill the most important role of a parent; the role of teacher. A role all parents must take responsibility for if we are to help our kids master the art of making "smart choices."

As a teacher, counselor and most of all parent, I encourage you to read this book and incorporate much of Steve's approach into your personal parenting game plan.

John E. Felton, Ph. D.

Note to the Reader

WHICH TAKES MORE TIME: trying to control your children's behavior, or teaching them to make responsible decisions? The answer might surprise you; it also might change the way you help your children prepare for their future.

This book is about teaching my daughter, Alexis, to make smart choices. I offer my experiences and the lessons I've learned so that more of us might help our children avoid the pain of poor life-choices and live happier, more purposeful lives.

I hope you will think deeply about the ideas I present. And if you agree with my premise that our job as parents is to teach our kids how to make wise decisions, then remember:

Children only learn to make smart choices by making choices

Introduction

A D A Y A T T H E S H O R E

EVERY SUMMER since she was born, my daughter Alexis and I have traveled from our home in Seattle to Cape May, a resort town on the southern coast of New Jersey. My parents and nine brothers and sisters rent as many charming Victorian houses as are required to hold all the children, grandchildren, wives, husbands and significant others for a week long family reunion.

To a worrying father, each new stage in his child's life holds its own peculiar terrors. This was Alex's fifth year at the New Jersey shore, so she no longer wanted Dad looking over her shoulder especially at the beach. I knew my job however: to catalog the smorgasbord of dangers available to my daughter and to prevent her from sampling any of them—especially drowning. As a child, I had spent each summer at the shore with my own family, so I knew them all: rip tides, under-tows, waves too big to handle....

Alex had grown up on Puget Sound, where the water is too bone-chillingly cold to entice a toddler into trouble.

Standing in front of our beach blanket on the first day, surveying our stretch of beach, I called Alexis over. She looked up at me with her blue-gray eyes as if to say, "What now, Dad?"

"Alex, let me tell you what the rules are, OK?"

"OK," she replied.

"When you are in the water you have to stay in front of the lifeguard stand."

She agreed.

"And see those ropes?" I said, pointing. "Don't go near them, because you might get tangled up."

"Okay," she said again.

"Oh, and one more thing."

"What?" she said, rolling her eyes.

"It doesn't matter how shallow the water is before the wave comes. It matters how deep it is after the wave breaks. It shouldn't be any deeper than the middle of your chest." I used my hand to show her where the middle of her chest was. "That's all. Have fun and don't throw sand at your cousins."

Then Alex ran into the water to ride the waves and I opened my beach chair and sat down at the water's edge to read The Philadelphia Inquirer. Occasionally I folded down the corner of my paper to check on her. Just as I began to dive into the editorial page, a woman sat down nearby in a beach chair along the water's edge. She had a little girl with her about Alex's age, standing impatiently while her mother put the girl's hair up in a rubber band. Finally the mom gave her a kiss, and I overheard her say, "Have fun in the water, Megan. Don't go out too far." And Megan ran into the water excitedly.

Then the noise level began to escalate. Every time Megan went further into the water her mother would yell, "Megan! Come in! You're out too far." And every time Megan strayed too close to the ropes, her mother would yell, "Megan! Get away from the ropes!" And every time Megan threw sand or shells, her mother would say, "If you don't stop that, young lady, you are going to sit on the beach blanket for five minutes."

It was impossible to concentrate on my paper, so I decided to watch Alex instead. You know how it is—a father can spend hours watching his five-year-old.

She was running and diving in the waves, enjoying herself immensely. Soon she and Megan were playing together. Then I began to notice something. From time to time, Alex would glance back at the lifeguard stand to make sure she was in the right spot. And occasionally, after a wave crested and broke, she would look down at her chest to see if she was in too deep. She actually held her hand up to her chest to measure a wave.

Megan was watching her mom. Every time she thought she might be in too deep or doing something wrong, she would look back at her mom to find out if her behavior was OK.

Megan was depending on her mom to determine whether she was in the right spot; Alexis was making that determination herself. Alexis knew what she was doing. And at least for now, on this beautiful, sunny morning, she was keeping herself safe.

One Saturday morning a few months later, back home in Seattle, Alex asked me if she could ride her bike around the block without anyone following her. I found my thoughts returning to that day at the shore. Blind luck and concern for Alex's safety had led me to define a set of clear boundaries for her, a safety zone within which she could use her own judgment. Now the same task (in the form of a bike-ride) was presenting itself again.

It might seem obvious to other parents, but I hadn't thought of it before: My responsibility for raising Alex extends beyond ensuring that she has enough food and a solid roof over her head. I am also her teacher, one of the handful of people in her world responsible for helping her learn to deal with the choices life will inevitably present to her.

I am also Alex's teacher, one of the handful of people responsible for helping her learn to deal with the choices life will present her.

This is not a book about parenting per se; it is about raising Alex. Children come in so many shapes, sizes and temperaments, I could never make the assumption that the strategies I used with Alex will apply to all kids. But

I do think some of the lessons I've learned have value for other parents.

I am not a trained child psychologist, nor do I have a research degree from any institution. My opinions cannot be supported with studies or long-term, in-depth analyses. Most of it I learned from my own mistakes. I'm just Alex's dad. I have taken the time, however, to think long and hard about this topic, because I care more about being a father to Alex than about anything else I do.

By trade I am a corporate trainer, working with managers of Fortune 500 companies like Nike, Eddie Bauer, Microsoft, and others. As a trainer I meet dozens of people each week, many of them parents, who seem to agree with the points I make in this book. (It's funny, but people who are new to supervising employees complain that the two tasks they are least prepared for are supervision and parenting.)

And I'll admit we've had our knocks as a family. Alex's mother and I divorced when our daughter was just two years old. Alex lives with Diane about seven months out of the year and she lives with me and her stepmother, Astrid, the other five months. Over a thousand miles separate the two places which Alex calls home.

I've learned my parenting skills from many people: my mother and father, Alex's mom, step-father and step-mother, and of course my own brothers and sisters. I am grateful for all their patience.

As I write these lines Alex is a happy, healthy eight-year old. While I know the journey of parenthood never ends,

I decided to put my thoughts down on paper because I believe I have gained some insight into these crucial beginning years. Other parents tell me that the teen years are the toughest. But I hope the foundation we've laid in the first eight will make the next eight a bit easier.

WORRIED FATHERS

Until that day on the beach, my approach to parenting Alexis was both a reflection and a rejection of the approaches my parents had taken with me. Like my parents, I tried to control Alex's behavior with a set of strict rules, but unlike my parents I was loath to punish her when she pushed the limits. Mom and Dad had employed a code of rules to establish control over their children, and when we disobeyed they punished us. I too resorted to rules, but I rarely followed through with punishment.

During my first years with Alex, I struggled. Was I too strict? Or did I give in too much? I was a Goldilocks in the house of the Three Bears: one bed was too hard, the other too soft. Unfortunately, the key to the room with the just-right bed eluded me. And unless I found it, both Alex and I would be the losers.

"THIS BED IS TOO HARD"

Alex and I perfected our roles at an early age: Dad made the rules; Alex tested them. Sometimes it even seemed —could a toddler be so savvy?—that she did things intentionally to try my patience. I often found myself playing the role of the dictator, the rule maker.

Looking back, I realize it was all a struggle for control —my control of situations with her. On one level I felt it was my duty to keep her safe. "Stay out of the street. Don't touch that stove." Some rules I felt were necessary to keep her from hurting herself. (And of course some were.)

But strip away that protectiveness and my need to exert control shot to the surface. It was much easier for me to frame a strict rule to control Alex than to take the time to understand her urge to "disobey." For Alex also had her own need to establish some control over her life, especially as she grew more confident in her own judgment and abilities. It was Alex's urge to explore that led her to test the rules. Disobedience per se probably never crossed her mind—not until I rose up to crush her.

Funny how she reminded me of how my brothers, sisters and I acted when we were kids. My parents were strict: "No crossing the street!" "No going out after dark!" Their rules worked well enough when we were too young to think for ourselves.

As we Reillys grew older, however, my parents' rigidity left us no room to use our own judgment. Binary rules leave binary choices: obey or disobey. Because our parents defined and enforced virtually all the rules, I felt stifled as I matured.

I faced a dilemma: On the one hand, if I obeyed I ceded control of my life to Mom and Dad; but if I disobeyed I faced the consequences—spanking, suspension of privileges, or worse, suspension of love.

Some of my brothers and sisters rebelled against the rules and directly disobeyed. Others towed the line and allowed our parents to control them. I came up with a third choice: I disobeyed and then lied about it. Often my choice put me in dangerous situations, but the freedom was worth the risk—or so I thought. I had few opportunities to become good at making decisions and not surprisingly, as a teenager I found myself doing stupid and dangerous things.

Binary rules leave binary choices;
obey or disobey.

Even toddlers need to stretch their wings, to put their own judgment into play. Choice gives children power in a world ruled by adults. Of course Alexis would test the limits of the rules I'd built around her. That was her job. The challenge for me was to stand back and watch a toddler careen along a sidewalk when she's scarcely learned to stand up! And I feared for her, the daughter of a son who'd had more than his share of lucky breaks. How long can you survive on luck?

"THIS BED IS TOO SOFT"

Was I too hard on Alex? Perhaps I was too soft with her—especially when it came to punishment. As she pushed the limits I'd imposed, my follow-through, my consequences, consistently melted away. It was always easier to dangle "one more chance" in front of her, or simply to divert her attention, than place her in the threatened time-out.

My parents knew how to follow through: Dad with his hand, Mom with her skillful playing upon my emotions. Perhaps because I remember too well both the physical pain of a spanking and the heartbreak of disappointing my mother, I found it hard to inflict anything like that on Alex. Yet I also knew that unless she experienced the consequences of her behavior, she could not truly learn to make better decisions.

Adults know — or should know — that the choices they make have good or bad consequences. My going easy on Alex might make her feel "loved" or "happy" at that moment, but it was lousy parenting.

" T H I S   B E D   I S   J U S T   R I G H T "

So I found myself as a parent pulled in two different directions, split between a bed too hard and a bed too soft.

The bed too hard said, "Spare the rod and spoil the child." Our responsibility as parents is to control our children's behavior — strict rules will keep kids safe.

The bed too soft said, "Love conquers all." Our responsibility as parents is to love and support our children unconditionally so they will learn to accept themselves. Self-esteem at any price.

How can we reconcile these two beliefs? How can we

nurture the freedom of unconditional love and at the same time exert the control that vigilance demands? To me these two paths diverged and I felt the need to choose one or the other.

We need to teach our children to get along without us.

I was searching for a middle way, and I had stumbled upon it that day at the shore. It was not an either/or proposition: My job was to love Alex unconditionally and keep her safe.

Yes, as parents we want our kids to grow up safe; and yes, we want them to feel loved. But more than that, our children need to develop judgment—their own judgment—so they can take care of themselves when we aren't around. We need to teach them to get along without us.

CHAPTER I

Building Responsibility

Good parents are our culture's best example of leadership...
Peter Senge, *The Fifth Discipline*

I HAVE NOTICED that as parents we tend to use one of two approaches to getting our kids to behave. The first is to try to control our children's behavior through the use of rewards and punishments. Those of us who use this approach will develop a set of good and bad consequences intended to keep our children in check. When the children are good, we give them what they want. When they misbehave, we punish them with time-outs, spankings, or some other display of power.

The other approach is to avoid negative consequences at all costs and to use rewards to bribe children into obeying. Parents partial to this system will reward children for their obedience and try to divert them from any negative behavior. The name of this game? Avoid negative consequences. After all, negative consequences are well…so negative. On those rare occasions when we do threaten our children with sanctions, we usually wind up taking a rain check on implementing the whole mucky business.

While both of these approaches may have some short-term effect on children's behavior, neither one helps children learn to make good choices. On the contrary: Both approaches short-circuit our children's attempts to take responsibility and make decisions. If I rely solely on consequences to control Alex's behavior, she may look to me—like Megan with her mother at the beach—to define the quality of her choices. On the other hand, if I go easy on her by letting her off the hook, how will she learn that as an adult her choices will have real consequences—that a happy life sometimes can come down to a few key choices?

If I go easy on her how will she learn that a happy life sometimes comes down to a few key choices?

The events that day at the beach presented me with a different approach, a third way. This third way—an approach that neither controls children nor lets them run wild—is made up of three elements that build on each other to help children learn to become responsible.

28

BOUNDARIES

A BOUNDARY IS A BORDER that defines or limits a specific area. The key word here is "limit." When I place limits on what Alex can have or do, I provide her with two factors critical to her development: safety and choice.

First, boundaries help keep kids safe.

Second, boundaries give our kids the opportunity to choose among limited options.

Boundaries shape our children's perception of freedom. It is popular nowadays to speak of "no boundaries, no limits," but look past the easy slogan and think about it for a minute. As adults, we know we cannot have everything we want; we know that choices define our world, and that the choices we make (whether good or bad) dictate the quality of our life. None of us live our lives without limitations—it would be impossible even if it were desirable. After all, without some sort of boundary in place, what would we have to burst beyond? There is a world of difference between striving to achieve some cherished goal, and pretending there are no parameters for our conduct.

Our children need a set of boundaries even more than we do. We at least have an image of the world—a story we tell ourselves (and others, if we can find anyone to listen) that explains "how things work." Children look to their parents for their first (and deepest) description of their lives, and their roles in the world. By establishing our expectations of their behavior, the boundaries we set help children to learn.

So if I give Alex every toy she demands, why am I surprised when she learns nothing about making choices? When we avoid placing limits on what our children can have or do, why do we complain about their low tolerance for frustration.

So was I too strict or not strict enough? With Alex I swung back and forth, avoiding setting clear boundaries one day, mandating too many hard and fast rules the next. Both approaches missed the mark; both interfered with Alex's ability to learn on her own to make choices. Lack of boundaries left too much judgment to her; inflexible rules left too little.

ENCOURAGEMENT

Encouragement helps children develop their own judgment to determine the appropriate behavior within the boundaries defined by their parents. Encouragement helps Alex realize when she is making smart choices.

Many of us excel at praising or criticizing but few among us understand the art of verbal encouragement. Praise is recognition for a job well done; encouragement recognizes progress regardless of whether the job was done well or not. And since actions often speak louder than words, we often encourage children more through our behaviors than through the words we use.

The act of encouragement gives children the heart to make their own decisions, and involves them in their own progress.

CONSEQUENCES

And finally...consequences. When Alex understands her boundaries and I have taken the time to encourage her choices, then she must experience the result of those choices. Sounds simple enough, doesn't it? Yet it took me years to get it. Either I avoided letting Alex experience negative consequences or I orchestrated a set of artificial consequences that I called "punishment."

When we allow our children to avoid consequences, they cannot possibly learn to take responsibility for their actions. At the other extreme, when we engineer and enforce artificial punishments, our children become dependent on us to define their choices. Parents must either let their children experience the direct consequences of their actions or present them with a logical choice before resorting to punishment to change their behavior.

BUILDING BLOCKS

Now let me again pose the question which began this discussion, and which lies at the heart of it. Which takes more of your time: trying to control your children's behavior, or helping them become responsible for their decisions? Most of us probably think the latter. But in my experience, it takes less time to help children learn to make smart choices. Megan's mother let her go into the water more quickly than I allowed Alex, but she paid for it almost immediately by having to keep fussing over Megan's behavior. (And unless Megan finds other opportunities to learn responsibility, her mother may also pay in the long run for her lack of a strategy.) I invested more time and thought initially, but that pre-work paid off — I had a few free moments reading the newspaper. It's like changing the oil in your car: You can put up with the minor hassle every three thousand miles or suffer the infinitely worse consequences.

By using boundaries, encouragement, and consequences, I was helping Alex learn to take responsibility for her actions and make better choices.

But it was not as simple as understanding the three elements. In order to help Alex develop and mature, I needed to realize the appropriate order and emphasis to be placed on each one.

The first and most important factor in building maturity is a firm foundation of expectations in the form of rules and boundaries. Boundaries build a foundation for learning to make choices; they establish the guidelines which help a child's decision-making process. Parents who want their children to grow into responsible adults will spend most of their time clarifying the boundaries within which they expect their children to live.

Once boundaries have been established, parents should spend their time providing behavior-based, encouraging feedback. Kids who know how they are doing in relation to clear boundaries can begin to manage themselves.

And if Alex has clear boundaries and encouragement,

then she chooses (remember, boundaries force choices) to live with the consequences of her choices. Parents who take the time to clarify boundaries and encourage their children spend little time enforcing consequences.

My responsibility to Alex is to provide safe boundaries and prompt, frequent encouragement. If I do a good job of providing these, then she will become responsible for herself by experiencing—and only by experiencing—the consequences of her choices, whether good or bad.

Boundaries...encouragement...consequences. Why is the order of these factors so important? Because it would be unfair to criticize or punish Alex if she had not first been told what behavior was expected. It is like forcing her to play a game without first telling her the rules.

To criticize or punish Alex without telling her what is expected is like forcing her to play a game without first telling her the rules.

For example, when Alex and I find ourselves in a crowded mall or department store, we invoke the "Line of Sight" rule. Line of Sight says both of us must stay close enough together to be able to look up and spot each other in the crowd. We first worked out this rule years ago when she was a toddler, discussing what it meant and why it mattered. We even made a game of it, popping out from behind clothing racks and escalators. I kept praising her, encouraging her, and soon enough she had accepted Line of Sight without question.

Sure it required some work up-front—setting the boundary, encouraging her to respect the boundary—but I have not had a shopping trip ruined in years.

Think back to Megan and her mother at the Jersey shore. The mother was giving a huge amount of direction, but it was all corrective. If she had taken the time to lay out some ground rules before Megan entered the water, then encouraged her to abide by those rules, both mother and daughter would have come away from the beach that day with far better memories.

One of my initial problems in raising Alex had to do with my assumptions. I assumed she knew what I expected; I assumed she knew right from wrong; therefore I assumed she was pushing the limits on purpose. Consequently, my main parenting tools became punishments like time-outs and withholding of privileges. Now I realize that before I punish Alex I must first look in the mirror. If I catch myself using consequences as my main parenting tool, then I am trying to control Alex too much.

For parents to help children become more responsible we must develop a different mindset. We must realize that if we expect our children to respect us, we must also respect our children. Rather than seeing our kids as good or bad, we must begin to see them as works-in-progress. That colicky baby screaming at two a.m. will grow into a cocky twelve-year-old poised on the precipice of adolescence. That toddler who won't stay off the stairs will be writing essays to half the colleges in the country.

Once again, I do not pretend to be an expert in the areas of boundaries, encouragement and consequences; I have only my own experience and observations to relay. I take comfort in knowing: that I too am a work-in-progress, and that as Alex grows and matures, so do my own skills and understanding. As I am raising Alex, she too is raising me.

As I am raising Alex, she too is raising me.

CHAPTER 2

Boundaries

*When I have a problem with the performance of my orchestra,
I get down from my podium, walk into the dressing room
and look in the mirror. Most of the time I find the source
of the problem staring back at me.*
—Leonard Bernstein, conductor, New York Philharmonic

VEN VIDEO ARCADES have lessons to teach. From the moment she peered in the doorway of Cape May's local video arcade, five-year-old Alex yearned to play…and play…and play. That first night Alex flew from aisle to aisle, touching every game, like a bumblebee who'd stumbled on a brand-new meadow.

I gave her a handful of quarters, and off she ran to play some games. Within five minutes she was back asking for more money. I dug into my pants and gave her a couple more dollars. She disappeared into the arcade, only to quickly reappear asking for still more money. I dug really deep this time, producing one more quarter.

"Is that all?" Alex asked incredulously. "Come on, Dad. I know you have more in there." I refused to donate any more, so off she dashed into the arcade. She was back in a flash. "Please, please, please…can I play some more games, Dad?" No, I said. Her begging grew more persistent until finally, inevitably, I got angry.

"Alex, you are spoiled rotten," I shouted. "If you don't stop begging, we're going right home."

Later that night I walked the beach alone, ashamed of my own behavior, repeating like a mantra, "The mirror, the mirror—look in the mirror." Look in the mirror, you jerk.

So then I knew it was time to establish some boundaries, and my wife Astrid (Alex's step-mother) and I sat up late talking over a better strategy.

First I apologized to Alex over breakfast, because I knew I'd been wrong to yell at her. Then I spoke the lines I'd rehearsed with myself back there on the beach:

"Let's go to the arcade again tonight, but let's do it a little differently. As soon as we walk in the door I'm going to give you five dollars for you to play with. That's a lot of quarters, but here's the deal, Alex—when your five dollars are gone, we'll head out of there and go for a walk on the boardwalk. OK?"

"OK, Dad," she said, and solemnly we shook each other's hand. We had a deal.

That night inside the arcade, Alex cashed in her five

dollars and quickly ran through all her quarters on the first game she tried. Upon realizing she was out of money she ran back to me, asking for more quarters.

"No, Alex," I told her. "Remember what we said."

She turned to Astrid, who shook her head.

Then she swung back to me. "Please, Dad, I won't ask for any more."

"I'm sorry, honey, but don't worry. Tomorrow night we get to do it again. Let's go for our walk on the board-walk now."

Grudgingly, she followed us—and within moments we saw she'd actually forgotten the arcade.

We returned the following evening. Again I gave Alex five dollars and reminded her we would leave when she'd used up her money. She ran into the arcade.

I watched her from a distance. She was walking around with her bulging pocketful of quarters trying to decide which games to play. (She was trying to determine which game would give her the most tickets—she loved getting those tickets.) The closer she got to using up her quarters, the more intensely she looked around at the games. She was trying to decide. Finally she was down to her last two quarters.

"Which one do you think I should play, Dad?" she asked in frustration.

"I don't know, Alex. Which game is the most fun and gives you the most tickets?"

She finally decided on Skiball and won a few tickets. Turning to me she pleaded, "One more dollar? Dad, can I have one more dollar? I promise I won't ask for any more."

"No, Alex. Like I said, when you're done, you're done. Let's go for our walk now...."

Children need adults to tell them "No." I believe they often want us to say it as well. When Alex stood outside the arcade pestering me for quarters, tears streaking her face, I think on some level she appreciated my not giving in to her. Those tears might have given Alex more control over her dad, but not over her life.

Children need adults to tell them no!
I believe they often want us to say it as well.

I admit it was difficult saying no to her and it was tough to watch her struggle with the choices she was trying to make. But that is the dilemma we must all face as parents. I love Alex so much it is painful to watch her struggle with her choices. But I would rather help Alex grapple with the choices she makes while she is still young. After all, how many years can we "control" our children? I expect I'll have Alex's attention until she is, oh, perhaps twelve years old. After that (maybe even earlier), other influences—her peer group, television, and (God forbid) boyfriends—will begin to outweigh mine. So I figure I had better teach Alex to make good decisions before she turns twelve. Attempting it later on would only frustrate us both.

Besides, when our children grow older, "Life" introduces

its own lessons about making choices. Learning these lessons then can be a harsh experience. I would prefer Alex learn them from me.

RULES OR BOUNDARIES?

BOUNDARIES DIFFER from rules. The purpose of rules is to control behavior. Rules are critical to keep children safe in areas where they may not be aware of danger. The purpose of boundaries is to guide decision making. Well-defined boundaries force children to make choices with their parents' guidance.

The purpose of rules is to control behavior. The purpose of boundaries is to guide decision making.

Some rules for children are non-negotiable. "No playing with matches" or "Don't touch the electrical outlets" are simply necessary to protect a child's health and safety. But if we look beyond those no-brainers, we see that the world of rules and boundaries can become confusing:

When does a rule become open-ended enough to be called a boundary?

What boundaries are appropriate for which ages?

What do you do when your own rules and boundaries clash with those of other people — your spouse, say, or perhaps your children's grandparents, or even the neighbors where your children spend so much of their time? Here's why I find myself often settling for rules rather than boundaries:

Rules require less thinking. It is much easier (and faster) simply to rap out an order—"It's cold; put on your sweater"—than it is to construct a set of linked options—"Here's your sweater. You can wear it if you feel cold, or you can carry it in your day-pack in case you need it later."

Rules are safer; they leave less to chance. Allowing Alex to exercise her own judgment often introduced a tiny element of risk. If she refused to don that sweater for example, she might become hypothermic, fall into convulsions, and die. Of course, the odds were a trillion-to-one…but could I risk it?

Rules make me feel powerful. Most of us relish the opportunity to tell other people what to do, especially if they are significantly shorter than we are. Rules are one of the tools I use to maintain control over Alex; they help keep me in the driver's seat.

The fact is, deciding to establish boundaries rather than rules for our children can be the toughest choice we make as parents, requiring all the decision-making skills we've learned over the years. But if I want my daughter to learn responsibility I have to take that risk. Forcing Alex to choose between compliance and disobedience may help me feel safer and more in control, but giving her the opportunity to make her own choices takes her own development to a new level.

The difference between boundaries and rules is the difference between humans and computers. Rules are binary, yes-or-no; boundaries require lateral thinking, fuzzy logic — they're mental stretching exercises.

Rules give children just two choices: obey or disobey. In these circumstances, Alex was guaranteed to learn just one thing — to listen to her father and become dependent on him to define the rules and monitor her behavior.

Rules are binary, yes-or-no; boundaries require lateral thinking, fuzzy logic.

The narrowest boundary is a choice between two options. This simple choice differs from a rule, though it may look the same:

"No playing in the front yard" is a rule.

"You can play in the backyard or inside the house" is a boundary.

In the past, whenever I used too many rules I usually ended up monitoring Alex's obedience. When I used boundaries instead, I could spend time tracking her progress. Using rules with rewards and punishments may have resulted in a more obedient child, but that obedience was only skin-deep. Scratch it and you would have found a profoundly disobedient Alex who obeyed only when punishment was imminent.

Let's look at some examples of rules I changed to boundaries with Alex.

Rule: "No yelling in the house."

Boundary: "If you want to yell you can go outside in the yard to play, or you can play inside without raising your voice."

Using this rule will force me to be the judge of her volume. The boundary encourages her to choose how she wants to entertain herself, without my deciding anything for her.

Rule: "Pick up your toys."

Boundary: "You have to put away the toys you are playing with before you start getting other toys out."

This rule will be enforced when I make Alex clean up her toys. This boundary will be enforced when she decides how to pass the next half-hour.

Rule: "In bed by eight o'clock."

Boundary: "You can go to bed by eight o'clock and I will read you a book, or you can go to bed by eight-thirty without a book. You decide."

Remember, in order for children to learn to make good choices, they must have the opportunity to make them. Choices also provide children with something else they need if they are to develop into responsible adults: control over their environment, control over their lives.

CONTROL, CHOICES, AND WHY KIDS WON'T EAT

THE NEXT TIME you find yourself in a mall, sit by the children's drinking fountain for a while and observe what happens. Most children who pass the fountain will at least try to stop for a drink. The kids whose parents won't let them get a drink often scream until the parents give in.

I once asked Alex about it. "Why do you stop every time we pass the water fountain to get a drink? Are you always that thirsty?"

"Not really," she replied. "It's just fun."

Here is my theory: Kids love to use the little drinking fountain because it is just for them. Adults can't use it— it's too low for most of us. And because the fountain is just for them, they have total control over the process. They can control how fast and how much they drink.

Imagine you are three feet tall, have limited dexterity, and must struggle to put your feelings into words. That is, imagine you're five years old. Now picture what that must be like. Adults make all your decisions for you. They decide what and how much you will eat. They decide when you can go out and come in. They decide who you can play with, where you can sit at the table, when you can speak and when you must be silent. You get the picture. That drinking fountain is beginning to look good. Why, then, do children often refuse to eat for their parents?

Note the phrasing here: "...for their parents." Because just about every one of us has experienced the exquisite frustration of hearing that our child "cleaned her plate" over at some other parent's house or at McDonalds.

Children—like all humans—eat when they're hungry. But most children will put up with a bit of a hunger pang if it means turning the tables on Mom or Dad…and controlling the situation.

Let's be honest. Children feel controlled at mealtimes because they are controlled. Most parents decide when, what, and how much their children should eat. Result? The irresistible force of a parent's spoon often collides with the immovable object of a child's jaw muscles.

Let's admit something else. If you can put food on your table, your children won't go hungry. My pediatrician once told me that getting a kid to eat is not a nutrition issue, it is a control issue. In our society, mealtimes are lessons in power, not protein.

Might there be a better way?

First, let us all agree that it is important that our children learn how to behave at the table. Let us further agree that if we believe in choices-within-boundaries, the dinner table might as well serve as our social laboratory.

No doubt you're wondering how Alex eats her dinner. First, she is allowed to help select the menu for the meal. She gets to pick two of the four items we have for dinner. (Thank goodness she likes peas, even if she insists on eating them frozen.) She can serve herself, but she must take equal amounts of each of the four items of that night's dinner no matter how small or large the quantity. If she finishes her plate she gets dessert. If she doesn't finish, that's OK…but there are consequences. You guessed it—no dessert. She can still have a healthy snack before bedtime (usually carrot sticks) but no special treat.

Alex did not become a good eater overnight. (Her

mother, stepmother, and I did not become decent parents the first week, either.) At first she took quantities too small to nourish her, so we would insist on a minimum (at least one spoonful) of each item. Gradually she began to eat more and more. Now because she trusts us and has some control, she lets us prepare the plates. She has decided she no longer wants to decide.

In our society, mealtimes are lessons in power, not protein.

Why am I belaboring this issue? Because providing choices for our children is not only key to their growth, it's critical for our own sanity as parents. When we present our children with choices—whether it is riding a bike, eating dinner, choosing a toy, or playing with friends—we teach them how to make better decisions, they become more responsible, they feel they have more control over their environment, and therefore they are happier. And the happier our children, the happier are we.

CONTROL, CHOICES, AND GOING TO BED

TWO BOOKS BEFORE BEDTIME: that's been the custom in our house since Alex was two years old. And it has worked well, until recently, when she began to balk at the idea of going to bed at nine o'clock — especially in the summer, when the sun sets so late.

"OK, Alex," I told her, "You can stay up until nine o'clock and I'll read two books to you, or you can stay up until nine-thirty and then read by yourself until ten. You decide."

"How about this," she said. "Can I go in my room at nine-thirty and read as many books as I want, and then you or Astrid come in right before ten to kiss me good-night?"

It was a good suggestion, and we went with it. But then another twist developed: At our family reunion at the shore, one night we all returned to our house about one in the morning after Alex and her cousins had spent the evening at an amusement park. She went up to her room, washed her face, brushed her teeth, and hopped into bed with — you guessed it — two books.

"Alexis, you know how late it is," I said. "We are not reading any books tonight."

Tears welled up in her eyes and she said, "That's not fair. If I knew we weren't going to read I would have come home earlier."

That stopped me. I could ignore her plea for fairness and enforce my will, but at the cost of how much credibility?

"You're right, Alex," I told her. "I'll tell you what: I will read the two books tonight, but from now on if we are out in the evening, you'll have to decide whether you're going to come home before nine o'clock and have your books, or stay out without reading."

"OK—but you are going to read to me tonight, right?"

"Yes, I will. But remember, from now on we have a new rule."

A few days later we were out to dinner when, shortly before nine o'clock, I felt a tug on my sleeve.

"Dad, I want to go home now so we can read," said Alex.

Once again I fought off the urge to control.

"Let me tell you what, Alex. From now on if you make the decision to stay out after nine o'clock, we don't read, but if I make the decision, we will still read the books. How does that sound?"

"Are you making the decision tonight or am I?"

"I am, so we will read the books when we get home."

She was happy and went back to play with her cousins. Of course, I didn't want to read the books when we got home because it would be so late, but I didn't want to leave yet either.

Should I have drawn a line and made Alex submit to my desires? Or would it have undermined the trust I was trying to build? Focusing on short-term behavior is a short-term parenting strategy. I may have gotten her to behave the way I wanted, but she would have learned nothing for herself...except that her father changed the rules of the game to please himself.

BOUNDARIES AND MATURITY

HERE'S TODDLER ALEX standing at the very edge of the corner of the sidewalk, her body drawn to the road, almost as if someone on the other side were pulling her with a string.

"Alex, you can cross the street only if an adult is watching you." Even this narrowly drawn boundary motivates Alex to ask her mother or me for help. I might have said, "No crossing the street," but I know Alex already is smart enough to understand "only if"—that superbly limiting phrase.

Now it's three years later. Five-year-old Alex has been aching to push the envelope, and I think she's ready. "You can cross the street by yourself only by telling me and then looking both ways." Voilà: the transition from a narrow boundary to a broader one becomes a tool for managing her progress.

Boundaries can be narrow or broad. Narrow boundaries limit the amount of judgment a child must use; broader boundaries allow for more judgment. The narrowest boundary is a choice between two options.

Narrow boundaries help younger or more immature children learn with more parental guidance. Broader boundaries help older or more mature children learn with less guidance. Narrow boundaries are choices defined by the parent; broader boundaries are choices that have begun to be defined by the child.

We start our smallest children with rules because rules are all they can comprehend. And as parents we need to feel comfortable setting rules, because children first must learn what a rule is.

While we may straitjacket our older children with boundaries drawn too narrowly, at the same time we can also torture them with overly subtle choices. Have you ever tried to reason with a two-year-old? I remember keeping Alex awake one night explaining how tired she would be at school unless she went to sleep. She gazed at me bleary-eyed, while I chattered away in my "foreign" parenting language. (Sometimes parents simply need to pull the plug on a situation without lengthy explanations. Alex doesn't necessarily have to understand my rules, but she does have to live by them. My job is to ensure that the rules I set are fair.)

The transition from a narrow boundary to a broader one becomes a tool for managing a child's progress.

I suppose some of you are thinking, "If that's the case, why didn't you just say no to Alex when she wanted you to read two stories at one in the morning?" I'm not sure I can answer that question. I know there have been plenty of times when I myself have watched a parent patiently negotiate with a small, uncomprehending child and said to myself in silent exasperation, "Oh for God's sake, just tell her to go to bed."

With rules comes the parental "No!" the Deny-er, the Taker-Away, the Gate-Across-the-Stairs, the Pick-Her-Up-and-Set-Her-Down-Elsewhere. When Alex was a toddler, I remember searching for a better way than simply saying, "No!" to her, to stop her from attempting something dangerous or inopportune. After all, I didn't want to sing the same nay-saying tune as my parents had with me. But in the end, "No!" made its inevitable appearance, along with diversions, distractions, even my ludicrous attempts to "reason" with her.

Alex doesn't necessary have to understand my rules, but she does have to live by them.

Alex quickly learned the meaning of "No!" She also learned how to fire it back at me—because "No!" (pronounced with classic two-year-old defiance) was her own first exploration of boundary-setting with me. As Alex grew out of her toddler stage, she developed more sophisticated techniques—sulking, arguing, hunching her shoulders—of asserting control and exercising her own judgment.

With this ever-shifting playing field of rules and boundaries, how can we parents possibly know what to do? We don't—not always, anyway. We try to think it through; we go with our hunches; we learn from our mistakes. That is why it is so important to spend as much time as we can with our children—for how else can we come to know what's best for them?

One day in the not-so-distant future, Alex will be pulling away from that same street corner behind the wheel of a live automobile. And if by chance one night she makes an error in judgment and I need to re-establish some boundaries, I hope I know enough to follow my own advice.

I might try to control her behavior by laying down the rule: "You cannot drive the car anymore" —but that would be poor strategy. Better to say, "You can take the bus or ride your bike until you show more responsibility in other areas of your life." (Or some such pious language.)

It's a narrow boundary—but a boundary nonetheless. And when she does demonstrate greater responsibility, I might broaden the boundary with, "You can drive the car on Saturday night until ten o'clock. If it goes well, we can loosen the reins. If it doesn't...well, remember, Alex, irresponsible behavior will have consequences—just like when you were a kid..."

DEVELOPMENT TOOLS

"No GOING OUTSIDE after dinner on a school night." As I grew up, that was one of the family rules we had to live by. Intended to ensure that we did our homework, this rule applied to all the Reilly kids under the age of fourteen. When we reached that magic age, each of us gained the freedom to leave the house after dinner—whether we were responsible or not.

While the rule kept us off the streets, it never motivated us to do good schoolwork. It did teach us, however, to find ways to escape without getting caught.

When Alex grows older I hope to use boundaries to leverage her motivation and help develop her sense of responsibility. Adopting or loosening boundaries can allow for improved judgment and maturity.

"No going out on a school night" not only would limit Alex's choices—it also could just about destroy her motivation. I would try a boundary instead: "You can go out for one hour after dinner only after I've checked your homework." This will tie her desire to go out with my desire for her to complete her homework.

As Alex shows progress and responsibility, I can loosen the boundary further—perhaps to something like, "You can go out after dinner until nine o'clock as long as you maintain your A average."

Consider the rules for going into a store most of us establish with our toddlers:

Rule: Don't touch anything in the store. (This invites rebellion.)

Narrow boundary: If you want to pick up anything, please ask me first. (For a young child)

Broader boundary: If you break anything in the store, it will have to come out of your allowance. (For an older child)

Or picture a child's learning to get a drink from the refrigerator:

Rule: Don't spill the milk.

Narrow boundary: Be careful drinking your milk. You don't want to have to clean it up.

Broader boundary: You can get yourself the milk — you're big enough.

(For an older child, the consequence — having to clean up spilled milk — is understood without having to be stated.)

The point is that it is difficult to use rules as development tools because they do not allow for children's using their own judgment. Boundaries offer the flexibility that both children and their parents need to promote personal responsibility.

It is difficult to use rules as development tools because they don't allow for children's using their own judgement.

PARENTAL AGREEMENT

WHEN ALEX WAS VERY YOUNG her mother and I split up. In the ensuing mess of our separation, divorce, and eventual remarriages, Diane and I wrestled with our pain, resentment, distrust and anger, while at the same time attempting to ensure a stable environment for Alex.

I admit it was difficult to resist the temptation to use Alex as leverage. And even though Diane and I agreed that we wanted "to do what was best for Alex," each of us had profoundly different ideas about what that meant.

You can imagine the result: endless late-night arguments over the phone, which left both of us frustrated and usually at an impasse. And Alex was the one who wound up paying the price for our injured egos and power struggles.

Because it was so difficult to rise above the inevitable pain of our divorce we enlisted the help of a family counselor who mediated between us on behalf of our daughter's interests. Over and over again the counselor reminded us of the importance of consistency and stability in Alex's life—especially when the most important relationship in her life was falling apart. If Alex felt safe and secure in both our households, the counselor pointed out, she was far more likely to develop a healthy, confident personality.

With the counselor's assistance, Diane and I painstakingly hammered out agreements on key issues: bedtimes, eating, television, etc. It wasn't easy, but gradually we put Alex's emotional health above our own damaged egos, even as we insulated her from the difficult nuts-and-bolts negotiations of our divorce.

Don't get me wrong: Alex was very sad when her mother and I broke up, but she recognized that we had found agreement on the things that mattered in her world. The agreements we reached established a unified parenting role for Alex, regardless which parent she was with. At first she wasn't entirely pleased that we both knew her bedtime, but at least she knew that she could rely on us, her parents.

The most important lesson I learned was the power I had as Alex's father to influence her life. Whenever Diane and I agreed on and enforced the same boundaries, our effectiveness reached its peak. Whenever we reached an impasse or wavered in our enforcement of rules, our ability to help Alex was undercut. At those times not only did Alex grow confused, she also learned she could manipulate us: "I get to do this at my mom's house—why won't you let me?"

And when Alex's life became unpredictable, she stopped thinking and deciding for herself because it was no longer safe for her to do so.

Before Diane and I divorced, often I would come home from work looking forward to seeing Alex. Having spent all day dealing with work problems, the last thing I wanted to do was to get tough with her. Just the opposite: I wanted to let her stay up past her bedtime and have dessert after she had ignored her dinner.

Her mother accused me of undoing the foundation she had been trying to lay down all day. "I have a right to spoil my child," I responded.

Eventually I realized Diane was right. My reasons for wanting to spoil Alex were selfish; I simply wanted to avoid the effort of holding Alex accountable for her actions. While I strove for peace and quiet each evening, I was ignoring Alex's need for consistency, stability, and not being let off the hook.

There is no more powerful team for raising a child than a pair (or in Alex's case, a team) of caring parents with a mutually agreed-upon set of expectations that are equally enforced. The reverse also is true: Parents who sabotage each other's work through discrepancies, misalignment, or unequal enforcement create an unstable environment for their kids, and weaken their own effectiveness as parents.

When Alex's life became unpredictable she stopped thinking and deciding for herself because it was no longer safe for her to do so.

And the process for reaching agreements is ongoing. Diane and I have regular long-distance telephone conversations about movies, TV shows, Alex's progress in school, etc. And we continue to argue. The difference today is that we both agree that a united front is more important than winning an argument.

Now that Diane and I both have remarried, the process of working out a united front has become more complicated. We are lucky that both of Alex's stepparents love her and put her interests above their own. Of course with more parents it takes more time to work things out, but then that is the price we pay for our complicated adult lives.

BOUNDARIES AND SOCIETY

THROUGHOUT THE TWENTIETH CENTURY every generation of American parents has come to feel that it has "lost control" of its children. Is there nothing new, then, in our current round of worrying about "the youth of today"?

I think there is. I believe there is one key difference between the panic of earlier eras and the crisis we now face. In other times parents and society as a whole attempted to establish clear boundaries, only to witness the up-and-coming generation blow those boundaries apart. Today—perhaps out of a collective weariness with history—the current generation of parents and grownups appears to have thrown in the towel, given up in the attempt to delineate expectations for our children.

"What's the point?" perhaps you are asking. "If each new generation of young people is destined to explode the boundaries of the generation behind it, why waste our time and energy in a futile exercise?"

Well, think about it.

If you push against nothing, you will fall down. It is a law of nature. Every young generation will try to break down the walls—that has been the task and the pleasure of young people for as long as stories have been told. At the same time, every adult generation has tried—must try—to maintain those same walls against too much damage. We do this not for ourselves; truly we do it for our children.

Our boundaries define the "walls" around young people's behavior. Of course these are not physical barriers, but a set of invisible boundaries that create the moral sense of good or bad, acceptable or unacceptable, right or wrong.

If you push against nothing you will fall down. It is a law of nature.

How does any society establish boundaries for its children? Through a combination of rules and expectations. For example, I expect Alex to say, "May I be excused?" after she finishes eating. I also expect her to carry her plate from the dining room table to the kitchen counter. These expectations take on the force of boundaries for Alex as soon as I have gone through the process of communicating them to her. Boundary setting, then, begins with me: developing expectations for my daughter's behavior, and then communicating them properly. Unless I perform both of those responsibilities, I shouldn't be surprised by Alex's behavior. She'd probably say, "Well, I didn't even know you wanted me to ask to be excused..." —and she'd be right.

This setting of expectations by a society is a complicated process that operates on several levels simultaneously. It starts with parents' expectations of acceptable behavior, then add in local (neighborhood) community norms, and top it off with national community standards.

As children mature into adults, their perception of what is expected of them develops gradually. Babies and toddlers pick up almost all their cues from their immediate surroundings: parents, siblings, close family members, and in many cases child care facilities. As preschoolers make friends, attend play groups, or spend more time in child care, they start to learn that non-family members have expectations of them too. Television, movies, magazines, and newspapers all add new ingredients to the stew of expectations; even the view of different neighborhoods seen from a school bus window delivers its own message about society's expectations. Each year brings new levels of expectations to growing children, with milestones along the way: the first day of school, learning to ride a bike, graduating to a new school. Some of these milestones will have more impact on children's lives than others. I fear Alex's first encounters with drugs or alcohol, her first sexual experiences, even her first credit card.

To abandon my expectations of Alex is not simply an act of laziness; it is irresponsible.

To abandon my expectations of Alex, to let her "make her own decisions" without my having established boundaries for her from the start, is not simply an act of laziness; it is irresponsible and sends as clear a message about my expectations as if I said, "Go ahead and shoplift that pack of gum." When we lack the gumption to establish clear expectations, other noises are guaranteed to fill the gap: television, consumerism, adolescent peer pressure…

That's my list, anyway. I expect yours reads differently. The point is, each of us has the right and responsibility to establish expectations, boundaries, within our families. If we don't do it, something else most definitely will—and whatever that is, it won't answer to you.

When we lack the gumption to establish clear expectations something else most definitely will—and whatever it is,

it won't answer to you.

CHAPTER 3

Encouragement

If a child lives with encouragement, he learns confidence.
If a child lives with praise, he learns to appreciate.
Anonymous

KNOW WHY American refrigerators keep getting bigger—to accommodate all those squiggly drawings and blotchy paintings our budding child-artists produce.

When Alexis was in preschool she would come home at the end of each day with at least one picture she had drawn for me. Beaming, she could hardly wait to show it to me, she was so proud. And caring, nurturing parent that I was, I always made a fuss over her artwork.

"Oh, Alex—it's a masterpiece!" I would say, trying to alter my remarks from the day before so I sounded more sincere. Then I would dutifully stick it to the front of the refrigerator among her other "works." Having praised my daughter to the skies, I considered myself a good parent who took an interest in my child's ability.

One day I was at a friend's home when her little boy, Chase, came in from kindergarten. He too had a drawing for Carol, his mom. Chase pulled it from his backpack and proudly held it up to her. "This is beautiful, Chase!" she said. "I especially like the way you used blue for the sky and white for the clouds."

Chase pulled the picture out of her hands to see what she was referring to. "Oh, yeah," he said nonchalantly, and handed it back to his mom for the inevitable refrigerator treatment.

After Chase had gone outside, Carol turned to me with an amused look. "Another day, another priceless work of art," she said dryly.

"That was good, though, the way you singled out one portion of it for a compliment," I told her. "You've found a way to make this incessant praise less monotonous."

"But I do like the blue and white at the top," she said. "I'll admit the rest of it's nothing to sing about, but I want to encourage Chase to do more of what he was attempting there."

Later that night I thought about Carol's "technique" with her son. This was praise taken to a new level: Where I simply recognized Alex for a job well done, Carol focused on the specific skill Chase had used to create the picture. My main tool for feedback was praise; hers was encouragement.

Let me say it again: I'm no "natural" when it comes to parenting. I put in the time and try to do the best I can. And when I observe good technique, I do attempt to work it into the Alexis Game Plan.

So from that day on I began to respond differently to Alex's artwork. I started to look for specific skills to reinforce. One day she came home with a picture from an Aladdin coloring book. I said, "Thank you, Alex. This is beautiful! I like the way you colored the Genie with the exact colors from the movie." The drawing wasn't perfect, but it was an improvement over her previous attempts, and that was something I wanted her to recognize.

"Oh, yeah," she said, clearly less impressed than I was.

The very next day she came home with a page from a Beauty and the Beast coloring book. As she presented it to me she said, "Hey, Dad, look! I used the same colors as in the movie. Remember?"

"Yes, Alex, I do. That makes it look really special," I replied.

I had to stop myself from adding, "And your daddy learned something special today too. He learned the difference between praise and encouragement—and it's going to change both our lives."

PRAISE OR ENCOURAGEMENT?

PRAISE AND ENCOURAGEMENT may resemble each other, but they have profoundly different effects on children.

Praise is results-based feedback. Praise is "Good girl!"

or "Great job!" or "What a pretty picture!" Encouragement is process-based feedback. Encouragement is, "That was something new" or "I like the way you get right back up and try it one more time" or "You're really starting to recognize those letters."

Praise focuses on the end result; encouragement reinforces behaviors or skills, regardless of whether the child achieved the end result.

And perhaps the biggest difference of all: Encouragement works practically anytime, while praise sounds hollow if it's used too often or to avoid giving a sincere opinion.

Don't get me wrong: Praise does have its place. In my opinion, though, we tend to overuse praise, and kids over the age of three often can spot it as insincere. Most of us use praise instead of encouragement simply because it takes less effort, or because we have never pondered the difference between the two.

Consider this most basic situation: Your three-year-old son has had a friend over in the afternoon, and miraculously the two children have played together smoothly for two hours. "What a good boy!" you say; or you might try something like, "Thanks for playing so nicely with your friend. It really was fun for you both."

Do the two phrases sound the same to you? "What a good boy" is praise; it's the verbal equivalent of a hug or a pat on the head. "Thanks for playing so nicely..." on the other hand, offers encouragement; it reinforces your son's efforts to learn and practice his social skills. Not only that, encouragement also signals to him that you have noticed those efforts of his. Imagine now if you hadn't encouraged him! A pat on the head is nice, but you still would have left him wondering what it was he'd accomplished, and whether (since pats on the head can mean practically anything) you noticed his achievement.

Here is another example:

Your daughter's team just won a soccer game.

Praise: "Congratulations! That was a great game."

Encouragement: "I liked the way you were passing the ball to each other. That shows real teamwork."

Your daughter's team just lost a soccer game.

Praise: "Super game—I'm impressed!"

Encouragement: "Your team had some great moments out there...like that time in the first half when you stopped the tall girl from scoring. You really held your ground against her. I'd love to see more of that in your next game..."

Did you notice how the "praise" was the same in either situation? That's because you can praise someone without thinking much about it—it's an automatic response. Encouragement, on the other hand, is more specific, and requires more of your attention. It's an authentic act of communication.

Your son has brought home a poor report card.

Praise (criticism): "These grades are terrible. I better see a change in attitude, mister, or you can forget about trying out for baseball."

Encouragement: "Well, I've seen worse. Your last report card, for example. Seriously, I'm really pleased that you brought up your grade in math. Math is one of those subjects that really tests a person's thinking; so this better score tells me that you've got a good brain in your head. Now I want to see you use that same brain with your language arts. What do you think needs to happen for you to improve in that subject as well?"

Encouragement is more specific and requires more attention. It is an authenic act of communication.

Parents who want to help their children learn to make better choices will find encouragement a helpful tool. Not only does encouragement help children notice improvements in their own behavior; it actually helps them manage their own progress. Encouragement also helps parents pay attention to their children's progress, by identifying their children's improvement, assets, and strengths. As I began to search Alex's pieces of art each day for aspects to encourage, I began to notice her progress. I had never before realized the rate at which she learned. My search for encouragement forced me to pay attention to her development.

EFFECTS OF PRAISE AND ENCOURAGEMENT

PRAISE AND ENCOURAGEMENT have different effects on children. Praise is designed to make children feel good, to reward them for good performance. Well, nothing wrong with that—we all need rewards. But that's all it is. Praise boils down to this most basic equation: You are a good child. Of course children need to hear this—but only to a certain point. And taken too far, praise can invoke the Law of Diminishing Returns: The more praise you heap upon your child, the less effect it has.

Let's look at what can happen when parents rely too much on praise alone. Children begin to see praise as an attempt to control their behavior through the use of a reward—to repeat the behavior desired by a parent, teacher or some other authority figure. It can be especially de-motivating to children who feel they performed poorly.

Encouragement works differently. Because encouragement reinforces children's specific skills or behaviors, it motivates them to look more closely for self-improvement. The result: self-managing behavior. When we encourage our children, they are more likely to witness their own improvements. Remember Alex's Aladdin drawing? I pointed out to her that she used the same colors as in the movie. The very next day she rushed over to point out to me how she had tried the same technique in her Beauty and the Beast picture. She was beginning to recognize her own progress.

Praise and encouragement are not an either/or proposition: they work together. While giving praise comes naturally for most of us, it may take a little practice to get the hang of offering encouragement. Praise can be delivered while we're on auto-pilot; encouragement is an act of communication. To encourage children, parents must pay more attention to the whole learning process, not just the end result. This takes more of our attention and awareness, but not much more of our time. And the benefits to our children make it worthwhile.

The more praise you heap upon your child, the less effect it has.

An encouraged child is a transformed child. And because encouragement recognizes a child's effort and improvement, kids can grow comfortable with the fact that they are not perfect. They can begin to accept that though not perfect, at least they are improving. Encouragement takes into account children's imperfections and their struggle to improve. "Great job!" can sound patronizing to a child who just lost a soccer game. "You passed the ball better this time," or "You worked really hard," sound sincere. Progress has its own rewards.

We must praise and encourage. While we try to foster our children's own inner motivators, we also must sweeten the pot from time to time with a treat, a promise, a reward. Part of the job of parenting is to customize the program to suit both our own personal style and our child's personality.

I can look back on dozens of instances with Alex where I might have or should have chosen a different strategy. The arcade episode, for instance: Once it was clear to me on the third night that she'd learned the lesson I was trying to teach, why didn't I give her another dollar just for a treat? Why did I choose to be so doctrinaire?

I cannot explain my own misfirings and miscues except to say that flexibility—like so much else in parenting—requires constant refinement through practice.

EVERYDAY ENCOURAGEMENT

As I BEGAN to realize the power of encouragement, I looked for ways to put it in play. I wanted to use encouragement with Alex to reinforce specific skills, behaviors and values.

Almost immediately I became aware of everything Alex was doing right instead of doing wrong. That in itself was an eye-opener to me. I discovered a disturbing tendency of mine to notice only when Alex was misbehaving, even though most of the time she was behaving just fine. (I suspect I'm not the only parent guilty of this.)

Now when I come upon her reading quietly, I sit down next to her, give her a hug and say, "I'm glad you like to read, Alex. It will make it so much easier when you get into upper grades." When I observe her sharing with her friends, I say, "Thanks for sharing, Alex. That really helps you all get along and have fun." When she cleans her room before going to school, I reinforce that behavior by pointing out how her action helps me manage my workload.

It is too easy for parents to focus on the five percent of the actions that our children do wrong and not the ninety-five percent they do correctly. Encouragement focuses on what they are doing well; it reinforces the values we want our children to adopt.

DISCOURAGEMENT?

Is DISCOURAGEMENT the opposite of encouragement? Not really; I prefer to think of it as the flip-side of encouragement. By encouraging desired behaviors I hope to discourage the opposite one. Parents who want to discourage negative behavior simply can encourage the desired positive behavior.

To discourage children's back-talk, I encourage (and praise) Alex whenever she talks to me with respect. To discourage messy habits, I offer encouragement when she makes an effort (however minuscule) to put her things away. Whenever she stays close to me at the mall I encourage her, hoping to discourage her wandering off.

In other words, show your children what you want, rather than berate them for what you don't want.

A parent's discouragement can be a hard hit to young children's self-esteem. As children grow older—and if bad habits continue—active discouragement may be necessary. As with everything else in parenting, there are no hard and fast rules.

ENCOURAGING VALUES

WHEN ALEXIS WAS SIX years old, her stepmother and I gave her a choice. On Christmas Eve either we could stay home and invite friends over, or we could journey into the center of the city to help out homeless people. It has since become a tradition in our family that we do something for the homeless on Christmas Eve.

One spring day Alex and I were downtown on another errand. For months she had been saving her money for a new doll she had picked out, and now we were heading to the toy store to buy it. A block before we reached the store, we passed a mother, father, and their small son crouching against a building. As we got further down the block, I could see Alex was struggling . She kept glancing back at the tiny boy sandwiched between his parents. When we reached the next corner she suddenly whirled around, walked back along the street, and placed her crinkly ten-dollar bill in the boy's lap.

She returned to my side, and we sat ourselves down on the curb. I was taken aback, and I asked her why she'd given the money away.

"You know, Dad, every Christmas we help people who have so little when we have so much," she said. "I guess I wonder why we only do it on Christmas."

As parents we have a tremendous amount of power to

influence our children's beliefs about right and wrong. Our words, and even more, our actions encourage certain values.

BEING WATCHED

WORDS AND ACTIONS can encourage negative values as well. When Alex was in preschool I had a hard time breaking her habit of name-calling. She would call her friends names, not nasty names, just kids' names, like "Meanie" or "Crybaby." I was always correcting her, encouraging her to "be nicer," explaining that name-calling was something that "we" didn't do. This name calling was not a serious enough offense to warrant a time-out; it was simply irritating.

As parents we have tremendous power to influence our children's belief about right and wrong.

Then one day I heard her refer to one of her friends as "Bonehead," and I thought to myself, "Hey! That's my word, not hers." "Bonehead" was my preferred term for reckless drivers on the freeway. Alex had heard me name countless Boneheads from her car seat behind me.

So she was watching me all the time, listening to me, learning not just from my words but from my actions.

And because she is full of curiosity, Alex's observations of me have led to some intense conversations — especially as she's grown older.

"My teacher says alcohol is a drug," eight-year-old Alex said to me one night at the dinner table, staring at my glass of red wine. "She says beer and wine have alcohol in them."

"That's true," I said. "They both do have alcohol, and alcohol is a type of drug."

"So why do you drink beer and wine?" she asked.

"They make me feel good," I replied.

"But isn't it bad to use drugs?"

"It's not that simple," I said, trying to choose my words carefully. I could tell Alex's questions came straight out of her drug education curriculum at school. I didn't want to undo the lessons she was learning, but I didn't want to feed her a load of hypocritical nonsense either.

"Some drugs are more powerful than others, so they're potentially more harmful," I told her. "A glass of wine or a bottle of beer contain only a little alcohol, and for most grownups there's not much of a risk involved. Some people are addicted to alcohol; they can't stop at one drink, and they drink more and more till they're drunk out of their minds. Luckily, I'm not one of those people, so I can enjoy a drink at dinner without worrying about getting drunk and losing control. Does that answer your question?"

She nodded, satisfied — at least for the time being. I knew that would not be our last word on the subject; in fact I hope we come back to it again and again. When our children start asking us these questions, of course each of us will have our own answers spoken in our own words. Just remember that lies and hypocrisy are easier to spot than…well, than a drunk trying to pass as sober.

CHAPTER 4

Consequences

You help me more by not giving in...
The Indigo Girls

LEX! Please make sure I'm ready before you jump into the pool like that!" When Alex was first learning to swim, she loved jumping from the side of the pool into my arms, and I would catch her just before her head went under the water. Now, for this game to work, you need both a child ready to jump and a father ready to catch. But Alex had developed the bad habit of leaping before I was ready for her. Time after time I would warn her, "Wait till I'm ready!" but then she'd "forget" and suddenly she'd be hurtling toward me.

Now I was angry. I dragged her to the side of the pool, hoisted her onto the tiles, and spoke to her sternly, my face

77

thrust close to hers. "Stop laughing. This is not a good game. If I'm not ready for you, I might not be able to catch you, and then you'll go under water…" But even as I was lecturing her I was thinking, She's not hearing me. She's not taking me serious…

So the next time Alex "forgot," I "forgot" too — forgot to catch her, and for an infinite split-second her head went below the water, before I pulled her sputtering up to the surface.

"See what can happen when you jump before I'm ready for you?" I said.

"Yes, Dad."

Ah, if only all the difficulties of parenting had such easy solutions.

Consequences are the final step in the responsibility process. There's a reason they come last. Because when parents place the appropriate emphasis on the first two steps, boundaries and encouragement, consequences are likely to be the least-used tool.

Before I apply consequences, first I look in the mirror and ask myself, "Have I taken the time to clarify boundaries with Alex? Have I encouraged her good behavior?" If I can honestly answer yes to these questions, then I have been a responsible parent to Alex. If not, then before applying consequences I must fulfill those responsibilities first.

But say I have done all that. What do I do if Alex continues to disobey and cause problems even after I have communicated clear boundaries and provided encouragement? Increase the number and duration of time-outs? Turn to punishment as a solution? What can I do when faced with a child who won't change her behavior?

Consequences. The only way children will learn to take responsibility for their actions is by experiencing the results of their behavior. Seems pretty obvious, right? Yet so many of us appear to have developed an unnatural (and hugely impractical) fear of allowing consequences to impact our children.

Perhaps an earlier generation would not have needed to hear this lesson—but we live in strange times. My parents used punishment—or at least the threat of it—as one of their main parenting tools. And it worked, too—at least some of the time. I remember not climbing onto the roof of our garage (age six), not shoplifting a pack of gum (age nine), not smoking a cigarette (behind that same garage, age thirteen), simply out of fear of my father's wrath.

Today many of us (including myself) tend to protect our children from experiencing the negative consequences of their behavior. On the other hand, we gladly let them experience the positive consequences. When children finish all their dinner, we reward their behavior with dessert. When they leave a barely touched plate, we find it difficult to follow through on our warnings.

When we do not allow children to experience the negative consequences of their behavior, we interfere with their learning process. We have to realize that they have a right to their opportunities to learn.

PUNISHMENT OR CONSEQUENCES?

THE PURPOSE OF PUNISHMENT is to control. The purpose of consequences is to instruct.

I have the urge to punish Alex when I am frustrated and want her immediate obedience. My threats of "big trouble" constitute fair warning: "Do this, or you'll wish you'd done it."

The only way children will learn to take responsibility for their actions is by experiencing the results of their behavior.

When I let Alex's head slip below the water, on the other hand, my intention was to illustrate the potential link between not listening and drowning, to help her learn that poor choices can have serious consequences.

Because I believe in the value of teaching children (rather than simply disciplining them), I try to use consequences whenever possible, and punishment just as seldom. But the difference between punishment and consequences can be slippery. I always ask myself, is there some sort of connection between Alex's behavior and the resulting consequence? For the more a consequence relates directly to Alex's behavior, the more likely she will draw a lesson from it, and the less likely she will view the consequence as a punishment.

For instance:

"Finish your dinner or no TV!"

That's punishment, pure and simple, because there is absolutely no causal relationship between eating and watching television. If I change the consequence, however...

"Alex, you have to finish your dinner because we won't be eating again until breakfast."

...the relationship between not eating and its consequence—hunger—becomes clear.

When parents use punishment , their children may surrender but they rarely learn much. Think of it from your child's perspective. What began as a reasonable request ("Please eat your dinner...") ended up as a bizarrely irrational demand ("...or no TV!"). "Watch your language!" degenerates into "...or I'll take away your Walkman!" Children delight in this type of behavioral non sequitur —especially as they enter their teenage years. The parent's foolishness becomes the teen's perfect excuse to challenge "the system."

The purpose of punishment is to control.

The purpose of consequences is to instruct.

Some actions are obviously punishments: spanking, time-outs, and withdrawing affection. Others are harder to interpret: In a more sadistic person's hands, a child's dunking could be a punishment disguised as a "lesson." It is parents' intentions that often determine whether we are resorting to consequences or to punishment.

Is punishment ever an appropriate parenting tool? In theory, no, for Alex is always better off experiencing a consequence that relates directly to her misbehavior. That's the theory, anyway; real life is less tidy. Punishment may not be "appropriate," but surely it is inevitable, at least to some small degree. As Alex's father, my goal is to respond more intelligently than my knee-jerk reaction sometimes pushes me. I may not always succeed, but at least I know how I'm supposed to behave.

It is parent's intention that determine whether we are resorting to consequences or punishment.

There are two different approaches I use to allow Alex to experience and learn from the direct consequences of her choices: Strategic non-interference and fork in the road.

STRATEGIC NON-INTERFERENCE

CHILDREN LEARN BEST from direct experience. Alex once touched a hot light bulb; she has never had the urge to repeat the experience. The burn helped her form a direct link between the bulb and pain. It was a powerful, direct learning experience.

When Alexis was three years old she had a very difficult friend named Katie. Katie told her she wouldn't be her friend unless Alex gave in to her demands. Alex was growing miserable, and she often came to her stepmother and me to mediate the dispute. We saw the situation as an opportunity to help Alex learn about relationships. We sat down with her and told her there was nothing we could do to stop Katie.

"We can send her home if you want..."

"But then I'll have no one to play with!" Alex said.

"That's true. We can make some time to play with you, but you might have to spend time entertaining yourself."

It was difficult to watch Alex struggle with her frustration and confusion. Finally, though, she had had enough. Katie told Alex that if Alex didn't steal some candy from our family goodie jar, she wouldn't be her friend. Alex told her to go home. We encouraged her decision; we also spent some time playing with her. But Alex was still sad and found it difficult to amuse herself.

Years later, the lessons learned from that struggle are still apparent. Alexis regularly displays the confidence to walk away from a classmate who tries to manipulate her by using friendship or approval as a weapon.

Strategic non-interference: Buddhism describes this form of influence as "actively passive"—letting people experience the direct consequences of their behavior by not interfering. Of course, responsible parents do not go looking for hot light bulbs to speed the learning process. For a child to spill milk while trying to fill her glass is an acceptable consequence; burning a hand is child abuse. Still, within safe boundaries parents can use the technique of strategic non-intervention by not interfering with their children's experience.

A brief epilogue to the story of Alex and Katie: At Christmas that same year, Katie gave Alex a stuffed bear, Scruffy, as a present. To this day Alex sleeps with Scruffy every night—he's her favorite stuffed animal. One day Alex surprised me by saying, "Dad, isn' it funny that I got my most favorite animal from my most difficult friend?"

The learning process is seldom easy or quick, and one of the greatest challenges we face as parents is watching our children struggle with it. We love our kids (sometimes to a fault) and it disturbs us to see them frustrated or uncomfortable. So either we minimize the impact of negative consequences, or we interfere with their ability to learn from positive consequences.

Have you ever watched your toddler open the refrigerator door, wrestle out the milk bottle and successfully pour a glass of milk? It is a triumph for the child and the parents. What happens if we step in and pour the milk for them so they don't spill it (or because the child won't do it our way or perfectly)? We take away their control and the opportunity to learn. We "enable" them to become dependent on us. Enabling is "help" turned harmful. We must realize that in a situation such as pouring milk, children learn a key lesson whether they fill the glass or wipe up the spilled milk.

But to observe this learning process—without stepping in to "rescue" Alex—has always been difficult for me. I try to be on the lookout for opportunities to utilize strategic non-intervention, and never to underestimate the power of letting Alex learn on her own without my interference.

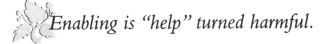 *Enabling is "help" turned harmful.*

Before I could utilize strategic non-intervention, first I had to learn how to let go of my own compulsion to smother Alex with "help." Often I would intervene simply because I could not stand to witness her frustration. I recall watching two-year-old Alex struggle to stack some blocks. After many failed attempts, she was starting to get frustrated; I could see the tension building within her as the blocks tumbled again and again to the floor. I felt she needed rescuing, so I sat down beside her and lovingly stacked the blocks for her. She immediately knocked my stack to the floor, then began stacking them again herself.

FORK IN THE ROAD

STRATEGIC NON-INTERVENTION can work wonders, but it is not the panacea of parenting. In some situations it may not be safe; in others it may not be enough. In both of these cases a parent may have to narrow a boundary down to a simple choice: change the behavior or face the consequences. In other words the parent and child are looking at limited options, stand at the fork and chose one road or the other.

When Alex persists with some inappropriate behavior, the fork in the road forces her to choose between changing what she's doing or experiencing a negative consequence. Whenever possible she makes her own choice, and so she learns to take responsibility for her actions. It also helps me avoid boxing myself into the role of the unrelenting disciplinarian.

For example, let's say a parent is faced with a child who strikes other children. This parent takes the time to make clear to a child that it is important to respect others. This parent also encourages the child when s/he plays cooperatively with friends. In spite of all this effort, the child continues to hit other kids from time to time. The parent has two ways to try to stop the behavior:

Control-based punishment approach: "Bobby, if you hit Jimmy one more time you are going for a time-out!"

This threat invites rebellion, because Bobby sees it for what it is: an attempt to get him to fall in line. Using punishment to motivate obedience is a last-ditch effort that too often degenerates into a battle of wills that no one can win.

Fork in the Road (let the child decide): "Bobby, either you play nicely with Jimmy or you can play by yourself in your room. You decide."

Offering children the choice of which fork to take leaves them thinking they are in control; at the same time it subtly pulls the parent out of the enforcer role.

Fork in the road helps children realize that their actions in life have results that cannot be avoided. My message to Alex goes like this: "All of us make mistakes, so I would never punish you simply for making a mistake. At the same time, we all have to live with those mistakes."

Not long ago Alex left her bike outside overnight in the rain. Prior to this we had talked numerous times about what happens when a bike gets wet, and I had given her encouragement when she put it away properly. Now I gave her a pair of options from which to choose: Either she cleaned the bike and re-oiled the chain (with my help) or she would go without riding it for a week. It was her choice.

Let's look at some other examples of the fork in the road.

Pre-teen refuses to clean up toys...

Punishment: "Clean up your room or no TV."

Fork in the road: "I need you to clean up your room before you go out this weekend. So you can take care of it now, or stay in the house until it gets done. You decide."

Teenager leaves dirty clothes lying around...

Punishment: "If you don't start putting your clothes in the hamper, we won't let you use the car."

Fork in the road: "It's a real help to me when you collect your dirty clothes in the hamper so I can wash them. You can put them there and I'll wash them or you'll wind up wearing the dirty ones when the clean ones run out. You decide"

The difference between "Punishment" and "Fork in the Road" may appear to rest on nothing more than verbal niceties and tones of voice: "You have a choice to make, young lady!" versus: "You have a choice to make, young lady."

What is the difference? On the printed page, absolutely nothing. But when I am talking with Alex, my tone of voice and my body language spell out whether I am truly offering her a choice, or simply signaling to her that I am about to flip my circuit breaker.

If I believe in the choices I'm proposing to Alex, then my sincerity shines through. I am prepared to help her learn. At that moment it's real, not a game: I am genuinely prepared to accept her choice, and am prepared—like her, presumably—to live with the consequences.

FOLLOW THROUGH

ALEX'S STEPMOTHER taught me an important lesson about consequences. Soon after Astrid came into our lives, I discovered she had an different approach to discipline than I did. Every evening when the clock struck nine, Astrid would bundle Alex off to bed. No "five more minutes," no "one last snack." When Astrid had her mind made up she was unwavering.

Frankly, I was worried. What if Alex grew to despise this harsh, unflinching stepmother of hers? For several months I hid Alex's copy of Cinderella; I didn't want her getting any ideas.

In the end, of course, Alex fell in love with Astrid; and not only that, she listened to her and obeyed her better than she did me. My concern turned to mild annoyance, and I asked Astrid, "Do you think Alex listens better to you than to me because she's afraid of you?"

"Why would she be afraid of me?"

"Because you're so tough on her. Why else would she move more quickly for you than for me?"

"Maybe it's because when you say, 'No,' you don't mean it, and I do."

"I do too mean no!"

"No, you don't," Astrid said. "When you tell Alex it's time to go to bed, if she whines you give her another ten minutes. I don't."

"Go on."

"And when you say she can't have ice cream and she begs you, eventually you give her something, even if you don't give her the ice cream. I won't, and she knows I won't. Why do you think she asks you for things rather than me, or when I say, 'No,' she turns and looks at you to see if you'll give in?"

"Maybe," I sputtered, "maybe she does it because she is afraid of you."

"That's nonsense," said Astrid. "She likes being with me, and besides, I rarely punish her or even threaten to punish her."

I fell silent; I had no more arguments to put up. Astrid was right: Alex pushed me because I allowed her to push me. Alex cajoled, wheedled, and tried to manipulate me because…well, because sometimes it worked.

And why did I have so much trouble enforcing boundaries and following through with consequences? Guilt, mostly: feeling guilty for spending more time on my career than on being a father to Alex. Guilt and the exhaustion common to all of us at the end of a long day's work. So when Alex would push the limits, my guilt and my weariness conspired to make me give in.

Here's what Astrid taught me: Fair rules call for solid enforcement. If I invoke a consequence, then I must follow through. So Alex chooses to wait until breakfast rather than finish the food on her dinner plate? So be it! Let her live with it. Giving her a snack before bedtime may make me feel less like a disciplinarian, but it throws off the entire process.

Fair rules call for solid enforcement. If I invoke a consequence then I must follow through.

I must let her experience the consequences. I can be proud of Alex when she makes the right choice, but I also can watch her mature whenever she makes the wrong choice. When I let her continue playing if she "promises to be good," or if I give her a toy so she'll keep quiet, I am actually teaching her to wear me down. And as her father I must ask myself what behaviors I am teaching when I let her off the hook. What is the cost of not teaching her about consequences?

No one seeks punishment, and children—like the rest

of us—will try to avoid paying the price for their behavior. At the same time, I do believe children want to experience the consequences of their behaviors. It may not be much fun, but it's real. And kids respond better to consistent rules than to wimpy, squishy ones. Consequences teach kids the difference between a bad choice and a good one, as well as where the real limits are in life. We owe our children that opportunity to learn.

CONFRONTATION AND CONSEQUENCES

LOVING AND NURTURING work best in raising a child, but there are times.... Oh yes, we've all been there, I'm sure: Confrontation Time. It's nice to think we can avoid confrontation with our children by following the advice in this book—communicating ground rules, encouraging compliance, etc. Nevertheless, sometimes even the best of us finds it necessary to "get in their face," as Alex puts it.

I can be proud of Alex when she makes the right choice, but I also can watch her mature whenever she makes the wrong choice.

She's a great kid, our Alex, but sometimes she makes mistakes. She knows she should show us the same respect that we show her, yet sometimes she slips up. Recently

Alex was working on my computer in my office, and I asked her if she wanted some lunch. "Be quiet!" she shot back. "I'm trying to do something here."

"Alex, look at me," I said. "You know we don't talk to each other like that." Her eyes started to fill with tears. "If you use that tone with me or anyone, you will spend time alone in your room. Is that clear?"

"Yes, Dad," she said, fighting back those tears. "But I was just—"

"I don't want any excuses," I stopped her. "I love you very much, Alex, but I won't stand for that treatment."

I know what you're thinking: "And where did she learn to answer back like that?" Okay, I'll plead guilty as charged; I've played Bossy Grown-Up in front of her enough to teach her the words, the tone, the works. Nevertheless, having made that mistake I cannot compound it by letting her rudeness simply pass unapprehended.

I never liked being punished by my parents, but I remember kids I grew up with whose parents never exerted any control over them. And if I had to choose between being raised by my parents' strict rules or my friends' parents' indifference, I would always choose my parents' mismatched system of rules and punishments.

CONSEQUENCES AND RESPONSIBILITY

As PARENTS we cannot make our kids more responsible; we can only create an environment in which they choose to take responsibility. Children are more likely to take responsibility when they understand that their choices have real consequences. Sometimes with Alex the process was unpleasant, but it helped her believe she had some control over her environment.

Back to the spilled-milk example. I can hear myself saying, "Spill the milk in that glass again and I'm going to get really angry!"

Will that work? Will my punishment make her more responsible? Well, she is afraid now; and if being afraid makes her pour the milk more carefully, then perhaps I can say it "worked."

Then you might ask me: "Did you really want to frighten your child?"

"No, of course not," I reply. "I simply wanted her to learn a little responsibility when she pours milk..."

I know what you're thinking: "Some people do want to strike fear in their children's hearts." Yes, it's true...and for those parents, this book probably has little to offer. But if you are a parent who feels guilty when you see the fear and confusion in your child's eyes after one of your "lessons," then I'm here to tell you: There is another way.

First clarify a boundary. "You can drink out of the big cup, Alex, but if you spill it you'll have to clean it up with a cloth." If she succeeds, reinforce the behavior with encouragement and praise. If she spills the milk, let her clean it up.

And if she balks? If she says, "No, I don't want to clean it up." Then I can apply an appropriate consequence to that behavior (perhaps by taking her old, now-abandoned "baby" cup off the shelf, the one with twin handles, sip-spout, and ducklings on the sides), until the lesson truly hits home.

CHAPTER 5

The Mirror Revisited

The road to hell is paved with good intentions.
Unknown

O YOU REMEMBER the story of Katie, Alex's young friend who caused her so much confusion and distress? Katie and Alex were the only young children living in our cul-de-sac, and inevitably the two five-year olds sought each other out to play together.

Katie's parents had characterized her to us as "a bit of a behavior problem," and said, "If she misbehaves, just send her on home."

Forewarned is forearmed: the first time Katie came over to our house to play I sat her and Alex down on the couch.

"Maybe it's best if we let Katie know the rules we have

at our house. What do you think, Alex?"

"Sure," Alex said, drawing her eyebrows together suspiciously. Why the lecture? she was wondering.

"I'll be working in my office so I need you to play quietly if you're inside. If you want to play catch or yell and scream you have to do that out back in the yard. Also, you need to put away your toys or games before you go out or start doing something else. And food is only allowed in the kitchen or at the picnic table out back. Do both of you girls understand?"

"Yeah, Dad," said Alex, who'd heard these ground rules so many times she probably could have recited them herself.

"If either of you keeps breaking the rules, I'm afraid Katie will have to go home for the day."

"All right, Mister Reilly," Katie replied, looking a bit shy.

"Great! Have fun and if you need me I'll be in my office."

The girls jumped up and ran down the hallway, excited to start playing. Before too long Katie was yelling at the top of her lungs, and I shuffled out of my office to talk to them.

"Katie, please remember the rule: you can play quietly inside or go outside if you want to make noise."

"Yes, Mr. Reilly, I'm sorry."

I returned to my office. A few minutes later I heard a thumping on the wall between my office and Alex's bedroom. I stood in Alex's doorway to watch Katie throwing a tennis ball against the wall.

Alex jumped up. "Dad. I told her not to do that."

"It's OK, Alex. It's just that I don't want to have to ask Katie to go home."

"I'm sorry, Mr. Reilly," said Katie. "I knew I shouldn't have done that." She was certainly polite about her disobedience.

Alex came to her defense. "Dad, she won't do it again. I'll make her promise." She turned to Katie. "Let's have a snack and go outside! Dad, can we have something to eat?"

I made up a tray of food and carried it outside to the girls, who were waiting at the picnic table. Then I returned to my office and made a stab at working, but my concentration was soon broken by some loud whispering down the hallway. The girls were standing in the middle of the living room, staring at a peanut butter encrusted cracker, lying face down on the carpet.

"I told her not to bring that in here!" Alex jumped in.

"That's okay, dear. Katie knew the rule and she broke it. Let's go, Katie. Maybe you can come back and play again tomorrow."

"I promise I won't do it again. Can I stay? Please?" she pleaded.

"I'm sorry Katie, but when you broke the rule three times you decided to go home…"

Before I started to write this concluding chapter I gave the manuscript to several parents to read. Those who agreed with the ideas I presented had a similar reaction:

"I just wish I had known this stuff before my child grew older," they said. "My kids are practically teenagers now. How do you apply boundaries, encouragement and consequences to older children who've already developed some bad habits?"

I don't have an easy answer to that question; nor do I have any direct experience to draw on. I have found myself in similar positions, however, where I used the same principles on a difficult child, such as Katie.

CONTROL OR TEACH?

MY GOAL with Katie was not to help her learn. That's a job for Katie's parents. I simply wanted to direct her behavior to the point where she no longer was disruptive. I did this for Alex's sake, because she really wanted to play with her, as well as for my own sanity.

Now Katie knew the rules but still she broke them, much as I did when I was a child. Most of the time I knew what my parents wanted me to do, yet I ignored them—not because I was a "bad kid," but because I found their set of rules confining and I figured I could get away with it. I suspect Katie "got away with it" as well.

So I defined the ground rules clearly with Katie, as well as let her know the consequences for not following them. And over the course of her relationship with Alex, she actually began to take my rules seriously because I always followed through with the consequences. While she never earned any merit badges with me for responsible behavior, she did get better at listening and obeying.

Following through with consequences seldom proved

convenient or easy. For example, Katie had a tendency to wander off whenever we went to the mall. As the parent-on-duty, of course I couldn't let that happen. I tried to touch all the bases: I took the time to tell Katie why it was important to stay together; I asked Alex to explain our "line of sight" rule to her. Then I added:

"Alex, you know what happens if you break the rule. Why don't you tell Katie?"

"If we wander off we have to go home," Alex recited with a touch of sarcasm.

Katie giggled; I doubted she took me seriously. And I was right: five minutes later she had disappeared into the crowd. I found her quickly enough, but I was determined to stick to my own edict.

"Let's go, Katie. You broke the rule," I said without emotion.

That was a field trip I'd rather forget. Both girls cried all the way to the car and continued to whine the whole way home. But Katie learned a lesson. I can't say we never had another excursion cut short by Katie's misbehavior, but it was a much rarer occurrence.

I know most parent's intentions are admirable. We sincerely want our children to grow into responsible adults. But becoming responsible doesn't just happen because we want it. To wring results from good intentions requires dedication, focus, and action.

I'm lucky that I figured out some of these ideas while Alex was young. Emphasizing boundaries and encouragement early on allowed me to avoid using consequences very often. I can see, however, that if Alex and I had a different sort of history together, our relationship might have developed in the opposite direction.

RISKY BUSINESS

MY FRIEND ALAN is divorced and raising his son John mostly by himself. Alan readily admits that when John was a boy, he rarely held him accountable for his son's irresponsible behavior. Alan was a loving father, an involved father, but a lax parent nonetheless, habitually issuing idle threats with no follow-through. By the time John reached sixteen, he had crossed his father's lines so many times without consequences that he seldom took him seriously.

To wring results from good intentoins requires dedication, focus and action.

One day Alan came home to a house reeking of marijuana. When he confronted John, his son blamed it on his friends who were visiting in his room. This wasn't the first time John had done something stupid, but it was the last straw for Alan. He told John that the next time he caught him with drugs in the house he would kick him out.

To John this was another idle threat. He'd heard it all before.

A week later Alan came home unexpectedly one afternoon to find a used marijuana pipe laying in the bathroom sink. Methodically, he collected John's belongings in a plastic trash bag and dropped them on the front porch. When John came home and found the door locked he was furious, but Alan held his ground. As he told me over the phone that night, "I felt if I gave in one more time I might lose John forever, even though I was risking the same fate by locking him out."

The next couple of weeks Alan agonized about his son. Where was he living? Was he eating? Was he safe?

For Alan, not knowing about his son was pure hell. But John didn't fare much better. After a friend kicked him out of his apartment, John slept three nights in his car before turning up stiff and hungry on his father's doorstep. Finally they hashed it out: John agreed to live by Alan's rules, and Alan welcomed him back. Today John has two jobs and he's applied to a local college. He and Alan still have their bumpy patches, but they have developed a true mutual respect.

I gave this book to Alan to read. "I wish I'd known this stuff before John started stepping out," he told me. He realized that the longer he waited to enforce consequences the more difficult and risky it became for him and John. And Alan freely admits that he got lucky with his son. He knows that it could have gone either way.

AND THEN THERE WERE TWO

WHEN ALEX WAS EIGHT Astrid and I were blessed with a child. Alex now had a baby sister, Madelynne.

Madelynne was the first child for Astrid and me, and we behaved like typical first-time parents. When Madelynne cried we picked her up. When she was hungry we fed her, no matter what time of day or night. When Madelynne howled for fresh air, we took her to the park. And when she wailed that she'd had enough of the park, we hurried her home.

After six months of this love-fest, Astrid and I decided it was time Madelynne learned to sleep through the night.

Armed with the best in parenting books and our own good intentions, we soon fell to arguing. As Madelynne's cries cut through the house at one in the morning, Astrid's heart ached and she yearned to go in and soothe her.

Yes, Astrid, the same Astrid who had taught me to stand firm with Alex; now was sounding a full retreat. And I, the same man who used to plead, "Come on, let her have it just this once," I barred the door to Madelynne's room, clutching my armload of parenting manuals, and uttered the heroic words, "She has to learn!"

The books had told us how to get a child to sleep through the night, but they failed to explain how a pair of exhausted spouses can reach agreement in the middle of the night. We knew what we had to do to get Maddy to sleep; we just didn't want it badly enough to work through our own issues.

Developing a unified parenting role is difficult because it takes discussion and negotiation. I call it engagement. You have to engage your partner to work it out. And with engagement comes risk—the risk of being wrong and having to give in and the risk of bruised egos.

But what else could we do? Argue senselessly and refuse to compromise? Confuse a six-month old baby with contradictory behaviors? Avoid the whole wretched business and just pray it goes away on its own?

With engagement comes risk—the risk of being wrong and having to give in and the risk of a bruised ego.

When we stopped to think about it, we realized we had no choice but to work it out together. And eventually Madelynne learned to sleep through the night. Until four or five in the morning, anyway.

Of course, this will not be the last battle Astrid and I fight over how to raise Madelynne. As parents we can know all the techniques and absorb all the advice we'll ever need and still fail. We can fail if we lack the strength and commitment to engage and work things out.

For if Madelynne runs away from us in the mall, if she throws a tantrum over quarters outside the arcade, or if we catch her smoking pot in our house, I hope Astrid and I have the strength—before we go blaming it on society, her friends, or even a chemical imbalance—I hope we have the strength to first look in the mirror.

Our Responsibility

The entirety of one's adult life is a series of personal choices,
decisions. If we can accept this totally, then we become
free people. To the extent that we do not accept this
we will forever feel ourselves victims.
M. Scott Peck, M.D.

 ECENTLY I FOUND MYSELF taking a walk with my
dad. I asked him if he thought raising kids in
the 1990s is more difficult than when he raised
the bulk of our family in the 1950s.

"I don't know about that, Stephen," he said. "But it
seems as though parents make it more difficult on themselves."

"What do you mean?" I asked.

"Well, when you were young your mother and I didn't

let the world intrude into the family the way parents do today. We didn't let you play sports that might interfere with the family dinnertime, and we had specific times you could watch television."

"Yeah, you and Mom were pretty strict."

"I know, I know, but we thought it was best for you. Today, on the other hand, it seems as though kids run the show most of the time—parents always shuttling them here and there, always giving them whatever they want. And I don't know any families which have a set dinnertime. Honest to God, parents seem to have a much harder time saying no to their kids than we did."

"Maybe that's because you didn't have as much to give your kids."

"Maybe. But I still think your generation could help their kids and themselves by doing with a bit less ..."

As adults we know that choices define our world. The choices I make (for good or bad) dictate both the quality and even the length of my life. My job as a parent is to teach that knowledge to my children. If children can have everything they want, then they lack any motivation to choose. Through making choices children learn to develop control over the direction of their lives.

But there is a world of difference between an indulgent parent and a caring one. I have come to believe that being strict and loving better prepares Alex for life than indulging her every whim. True love means giving Alex what she truly needs.

Let's face it. Love is essential in raising a well-adjusted

child, but it doesn't necessarily teach kids how to handle most of life's interactions. Nor does indulgence. Love teaches kids that the world can be a wonderful and beautiful place, but it doesn't acquaint them with its dangers, its competitiveness. It does not teach them that the difference between a happy, contented life and a life of struggle can come down to making a few key choices.

True love means giving Alex what she truly needs.

As parents our key choice may well be to spend time with our children, to be there for them as they grow up. After all, life passes us by much more quickly than any of us wants. Do we want to be startled by the sudden appearance of a teenager at the breakfast table? Or do we want to slow down time, to savor our children's development, and be their guides on their journey?

At the time Alex was born, I was a manager in a large corporation. My first priority was work; family issues ran a distant second. I faced a dilemma: If I wanted to remain true to my job — working long hours, traveling frequently — then someone else would have to teach Alex about the world. On the other hand, if I chose to become involved in her upbringing, I mean really involved, then my career inevitably had to suffer.

Well, you know the ending to this story. Eventually my

supervisor grew tired of my leaving work at five o'clock every day to pick Alex up at child-care. He became fed up with accommodating my travel schedule and other work obligations around my daughter's school plays and child care. He began to question my "motivation," my "dedication"...and in the end we "separated due to philosophical differences," as he put it.

Choices and their consequences. Those were tough times both emotionally and financially, but we made it through. And in the end, the consequences became rewards which I never stop reaping.

How ironic: I write a book about teaching kids to make smart choices, when the choice which most impacted Alex's life was the one I made. If we choose to stay involved in our children's lives, paying attention to their needs and trying to understand them, we have chosen to teach them ourselves. But if we choose work over family, material things over relationships, then we have abdicated the teaching to the culture around us.

Which do you choose?

If we choose work over family, material things over relationships, then we abdicate the teaching to the world around us.

Which do you choose?